EXPERIENCE

MEXICAN JAIL!

An Accidental Tourist Guide

The Unnamed Press
P.O. Box 411272
Los Angeles, CA 90041

Published in North America by The Unnamed Press.

1 3 5 7 9 10 8 6 4 2

ISBN: 978-1-939419-835

Library of Congress Control Number: available upon request.

This book is distributed by Publishers Group West

Book Design & Typeset by Jaya Nicely
Illustration by Alycea Tinoyan

Permissions inquiries
may be directed to info@unnamedpress.com.

I'd like to dedicate this book to my parents and all of the people who helped me along the way. Thanks so much for making a difficult situation easier! I am also grateful for the friends I made living in another country. I wish we had all met under different circumstances but everything happens for a reason and I am very happy that our paths crossed. (Not all the people I met of course, some of them were right bastards.)

CHECKING IN

My Phone
(somebody else's crack)

Embrace Your Mexican Jail Experience!

Just to answer the question on everyone's mind: Why do I get to write a guidebook about *La Carcel*? Well, I've spent over four years here, that's why. Prior to being an inmate, I was just a regular guy having a good time in Cancún. Without getting into the details, let's just say I assisted others with having a good time in Cancún too. But as I've learned, sometimes chilling on the inside can be just as fun as chilling on the outside. All you need is the right attitude, and some top-notch insider tips—which is where I come in. Everything I learned, I typed into my trusty Nokia 6500c with my two thumbs. I sent long letters to all my friends this way, even the ones who didn't send me any money.

Getting to Mexican Jail

Getting to Mexican Jail is easy and kind of magical. Like snowflakes, no two trips are exactly alike. If you plan on spending more than a weekend or two, you should consider how you get there, as that will determine the length of your stay.

By Air

Romaniak (from Romania), had 979 grams of his cocaine stolen by the cops at the Cancún airport, leaving him with 21 grams: the minimum to get 10 years in jail. Oops.

By Sea

Six Colombians were stuck on a broke-down boat off the coast of Cuba when the Mexican Navy showed up, which was lucky for them. But then the Navy blamed them for the literal ton of drugs they'd discovered floating nearby. Not so lucky.

By Referral

Delroy and Shantal, from New York, got here because Delroy found a ring on the floor of a Cancún jewelry shop and said to himself "finders keepers." The shop owner disagreed.

Resort Package

Fred, the retired USAF Major, who says he's also a doctor (though we're not sure if we believe that because Fred is a major liar), got here by pretending to be a guest at a resort. Nobody likes a freeloader.

Canada

Richard (a Canadian) is here for 20 kilos of marijuana and a few ounces of hash. He had a restaurant and youth hostel back in Guatemala and lost it all. Point is: you can even get to Mexican Jail if you're Canadian.

Take Lots of Pictures!

Mexican Jail is like a crappy small town. Not very picturesque, but everybody is up in each other's business. So feel free to take lots of pictures. I've included a lot of my own pictures; again, using my Nokia 6500c. Now you probably think that handsome guy on the opposite page is me. Well, sorry to disappoint. It's actually a picture of Jesús Malverde. *Señor* Malverde is the patron saint of drug dealers in the Mexican state of Sinaloa and people love him here. Paintings of this dude are all over Mexican Jail. Seriously, check him out. He's in Wikipedia and everything. Soon, you'll be taking your own pictures.

Jesús Malverde

Jail

You will be greeted by a guy called Hercules, who is a big bastard.

Hercules sits in a chair behind a big desk in the *oficina* of Mexican Jail. He'll ask you what you're here for and you'll say something like, "I'm here for the drugs you found." And he'll say something like, "How much drugs?" And you should probably say, "I don't know." "Ok, hold on," he'll say, and then he'll send this little guy off somewhere to get something. The little guy will come back with a newspaper. Then Hercules will start laughing and point to the picture in the newspaper and say *El Presidente.* The little man will probably start laughing too. It's very important to not laugh too hard, but just enough to show them you're a good sport. Everyone likes a good sport, (especially in Mexican Jail).

Local headlines will probably shout: "International drug ring busted!"

Don't take it personally. Not even if there is a picture of you, your condo, and your dining room table (with a lot of drugs on it). Hercules might think that you are in charge of this "drug ring." Which is why he is calling you *El Presidente*. So be prepared for Hercules to write down a number on a scrap of paper. Read it carefully. The number will probably be in the mid-four figures but don't be surprised if it is more. This is how much your stay will cost. Just like any vacation, you're going to have to budget for it. Then Hercules will offer you a phone to make calls. To make sure you get the most out of your stay, it is important to have ready access to cash on the outside, although it's also important not to overpromise. Sometimes, it's hard to track down friends from Mexican Jail.

Don't miss out on haggling with Hercules!

Just like a swap meet, haggling isn't just ok, it's expected. In fact, Hercules would probably be a little insulted if you didn't. When you tell him $5,000 is way too much, Hercules will say, "OK, come with me." Then he'll take you around back and show you a hole in the concrete with guys down in the hole lifting buckets of gray water out. The hole is full of sewer water. One guy passes a bucket up, hands it to someone, and they run off. The smell is terrible. (Don't worry about offending anyone if you happen to puke—they'll just make one of those guys clean it up!) "OK, *Mr. Presidente*," Hercules will say. "If you don't pay, here is where you work… all day long." This is when you will embrace the situation, and your new nickname. "Let the *Presidente* make a phone call," you will probably say.

∼ Savvy Prisoner ∼
Tip Numero 1: Pack Light

Hercules is going to take everything at check-in.
But don't worry, you can buy it all back later!

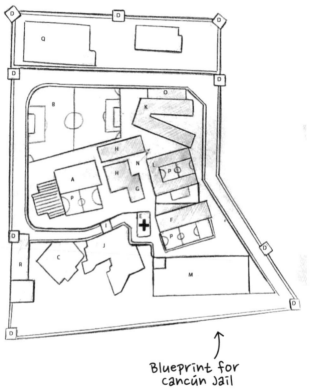

Blueprint for
cancún Jail

Getting Around Mexican Jail

A-Cuadro/Main Jail Block (massages available)

B-Campo de Fútbol/Soccer Field

C-Cubículo/Where you meet your lawyer

D-Torres de Guardia/Guard Tower

E-Enfermería/Medical services

F-Femenil/Woman's jail

G-Where some of my best friends live

H-Conyugal/Conjugal

I-Caseta/Guard's Hangout

J-Juzgados/Court & Admin Office

K-Almoloya/People lived here

L-Preventiva/Mos Eisley Spaceport (basically)

M-Sentenciados/Where you will probably live
(nice jungle view)

N-Capilla/Church
Where criminals make promises they can't keep.

O-Gym/Actual Gym
Where I was able to go to work on physical fitness.

P-Cancha de Basket/Basketball Court (dance hall)

Q-Mafia House

R-Rancho/Canteen (don't eat there)

My plancha with
folded laundry

Six important words to know that aren't *Carcel*[*]

Tepache: Homemade beer.

Talacho: Forced laborer, unable to pay the bribe at check-in.

Plancha: Concrete bed. If you have some money you can buy a mat and put up some sheets to make curtains.

Revisión: When the Federales or military come to check the jail.

Conjugal: The room where you and a visitor (or a prostitute-inmate) can have sex.

Fabuloso: A liquid soap. It smells nice at first but eventually you won't like it because everyone uses it as an air freshener.

[*] I would have included *carcel*, but I already gave you that one.

Being as polite as possible
will make up for your
lack of vocabulary.

Everybody in Mexican Jail speaks at least two phrases of English that you will understand. That's a good start! Those two phrases are, in order: "Suck my dick" and "Fuck you." So every morning when you pass someone feeling friendly you will probably get a "Suck my dick" which you should ignore, followed by a "Fuck you", which you should also ignore. When you first get here you will get no less than fifteen "Suck my dicks" and ten "Fuck yous" before breakfast.

Just in case you want to send me money:

1. Go to Walmart.

2. Ask for a MoneyGram to Cancún.

3. Send the money to Juan Francisco Trujillo. He is a taxi driver that has a service for the people here in jail. Great guy and very honest. Whatever you can send would be a big help. I am trying to open a candy store and need some startup capital!

ACCLIMATING

In Mexican Jail, chocolate cake sort of makes people friendlier.

One day in Mexican Jail, while I'm waiting in the *oficina* for my extortion money to clear, a chocolate cake comes in. Not a whole one—just two pieces. Meanwhile, Hercules thinks he will make a joke of me reading my book by taking a bigger book and sticking it close to his face. While Hercules is doing this he can't see me, so I take the plate with the two pieces of cake and hide it. This makes the other guys in the *oficina* laugh super hard. Once Hercules figures it out, he's laughing too. Later on it's just me and Hercules in the *oficina*. And out of the blue he offers me some cake and I have a bite. He starts eating a piece too, but for some reason, decides to give both pieces to me. Which is great, because I love cake.

Start planning your baby tattoo.

Guys in Mexican jail love their kids. Maybe not enough to be law abiding citizens but just enough to tattoo the baby's face on their body. They take a picture, copy it on their shoulder or calf, then trace it with a tattoo gun. Every single guy here ends up having their beloved baby looking like a fat bald man or a funny looking half human/half ferret. It's not the artist's fault, it's just that, as everyone knows, it's hard to capture a baby's features on a grown man's body. I just don't see the point. The kid isn't going to look like a baby forever and all babies look the same anyway (unless they are really ugly). I guess they don't realize the tattoos look crappy, but then again nobody thinks their own kid is ugly either.

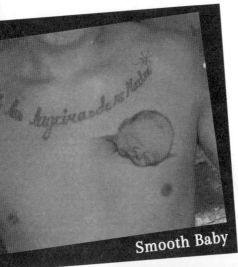

Smooth Baby

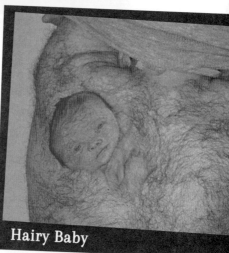

Hairy Baby

cuban Flag
(R.I.P. Mr. castro)

Holy shit! Did you know about Cuban Healthcare?

The Cubans here told me health care in Cuba is the bomb. What Michael Moore says about Cuban healthcare must be true. One guest told me he has never had bad service. Another guest said that when he lived in Cuba it seemed like everyone he met was a doctor. The school system is free and since everyone must go they most often go on to become doctors. He also said that the medical program and equipment is so good that people all over the world go to study there. Now the problem with Cuba is that there is no money, thanks to the USA. That is why they try to leave. Everyone gets what they need but no one has money except a select few. I've never been there, but I hear that everyone's house smells like gasoline, because everyone is poaching gasoline from each other and selling it on the black market.

Should I ask my cellmate what happened to his mangled ear?

Once you pay your bribe, you will move into your cell. If you have paid the full amount you won't have to dredge the sewer. But you will have to share a cell with six to eight other guests.

These guests will include *talachos*, *crackheads*, and the cell boss. A guy in your cell might have part of his ear missing. Not missing like a birth defect. More like missing because someone who was just a little bit too hungry got a little bit too close to his ear. I guess it could be a birth defect; I don't really know because I'm not an ear expert (or doctor for that matter). You could ask, but I probably wouldn't.

Language barriers are probably a good thing in Mexican Jail.

Along with missing a part of his ear, one of my cell mates also had two large bumps on his back. Large like a little larger than the size of a big marble. The doc lanced them the other day so they are gone whatever they were. This guy also knows four English phrases which he likes to impress me with and they are: *fuck you*, *suck my dick*, *thank you very much*, and *son of a bitch*. He says them every time he sees me. I would like to smack him sometimes but if I tell him they are really bad words he will just say them more and teach his friends. So I just ignore him and am grateful for the language barrier, which in this case is probably a good thing.

Don't forget
the balloons

A party is a great way to break the ice with your cell mates.

Parties are very popular in Mexican Jail. Whether it's Valentines Day, Father's Day or because someone came back to jail, parties are a very important aspect of Mexican Jail. If you don't care for crowds, noise, drugs or *tepachi*, then maybe a Mexican Jail party is not for you. Also if you don't like cock fighting. Here are some of the things you might want to include for your party:

- Greased pole
- Rotating dart board
- Two bags of cocaine
- Bottle of tequila
- Fighting roosters (two minimum)
- Drug piñata
- Raffle tickets and prizes like joints or an hour in the conjugal room

A Peso

~Savvy Prisoner~
Tip Numero 2:
Hang on to your Peso

The other day I drop a peso on the floor of my cell. The guy who picks it up is playing cards and because it's nighttime he's sitting around in his boxers. So far, so normal. Then he does something special. He pulls out his dick and tucks the coin into his foreskin. Then he throws it at me. I had to wash it. I needed that peso.

ARTS & ENTERTAINMENT

Jail librarians have
the best stories.

Julio got done for murder. Real nice guy and he supposedly didn't actually kill the guy. According to Julio the guy wanted to kill himself and he asked Julio to make it look like he was murdered by trashing his apartment and then he was to take the gun after he shot himself. Julio told him that was a very bad idea and that if he would just wait one minute he would help him sort out his problems but first he needed to take another hit of crack. Julio was puffing away when the gun went off. He picked the gun up and the first thought in his brain was: "I could sell it and get more crack." Today Julio is the jail librarian!

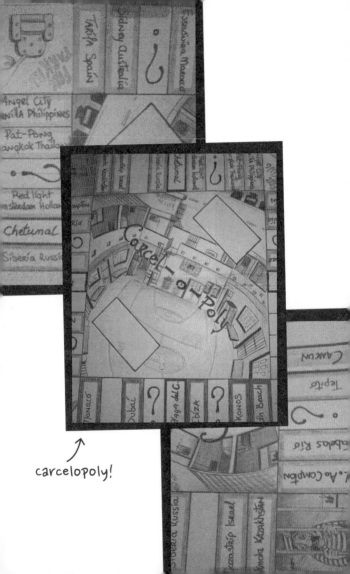

carcelopoly!

Sorry Hasbro.

If you want to play Monopoly this guy named Angel will want $200 pesos for his used set, which is missing pieces. My buddy Julio used to have Tourista, which is like a Mexican version of Monopoly only they use countries as the properties that you buy and you get deported instead of going to jail. But he sold it to someone for crack. So make your own version. Use your own personal situations for the community chest and chance cards. For example, instead of "A bank error gives you $10," do "Rob a bank, get $10." Loris, the Italian prisoner here, drew the board for us. Maybe he can draw it for you too. We called our version Carcelopoly!

～Savvy Prisoner～
Tip Numero 3: Play catch with the Mafia Boss

The mafia boss likes to hit softballs. If you catch one you win $50 pesos. (Don't worry, no one will think you are a suck up.) It's his way of giving back to the people he extorts and makes slaves of.

Jails in Mexico like to keep pets. My jail has an ocelot and alligators, plus goats, pigs, dogs and turtles. Who knows what your jail will have!

Slapping is pretty popular
in Mexican Jail.

There is a guy who went free and just came back. As a welcoming party they made him come out in the hallway so everyone could slap him on the back. Some used their hand while others used their shoe but some guys really gave him some licks. One even punched him in the face. It must have hurt.

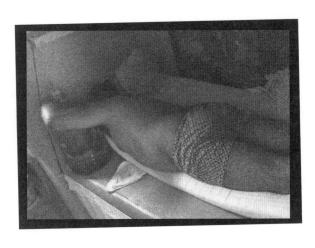

Not doing anything in Mexican Jail is like an activity too.

There is so much to do in Mexican Jail! You can be active in sports, knitting, drugs, dancing, or invest your time in an entrepreneurial pursuit. (I, for one, am considering the candied apple business.) Some people, on the other hand, don't do anything. They never leave their cells unless they have to for some reason, like going to the bathroom. You have to *try* to do that in Mexican Jail. Some people go to the bathroom a lot. I know somebody here who takes a dump every two hours. Good looking guy too, not counting his digestive system.

Spitting isn't cool anymore in Mexican Jail.

Spitting isn't allowed, which is good because people will just spit anywhere they please. People still do it when others aren't around, including me. The other morning around 5 AM I had to spit and I was feeling lazy so I spit out my window into the hallway but at an angle and with a bit too much force and it happened to make it into the cell across from mine. Right in the door! I know I shouldn't spit in the hallway but they wash the floor every day at 7 AM with soap and bleach. I guess you'll have to make your own decisions about spitting.

Maybe I should have mentioned this sooner...

Before going any further, it is important to point out that a bribe is essential for you to have a comfortable stay in Mexican Jail, which is controlled by a gang called the Zetas. If you cannot pay, there is not much need to read the rest of this guide. You are shit out of luck and it will probably make you feel pretty shitty to keep reading it.

Zeta Logo

Just who are these Zetas?

Mexican Jail is operated by the Zetas. Wikipedia says "Los Zetas are a Mexican criminal syndicate, considered by the US government to be 'the most technologically advanced, sophisticated, and dangerous cartel operating in Mexico.'" Even if the Zetas here don't seem exactly advanced or sophisticated, you kind of have to take their word for it, because they are definitely dangerous. The cartel is named Los Zetas after its first commander, Arturo Guzmán Decena, whose Federal Judicial Police radio ID was "Z.1." Zeta is the sixth letter of the Greek alphabet. It's also the word for the letter "z" in Spanish. Kind of like how the British call "z" Zed. Seems kind of silly, giving names to letters, but who am I to judge?

Not my candied apple,
but close!

"Beware the hobby that eats."

Benjamin Franklin said that, but clearly he's never been to Mexican Jail. One of my favorite hobbies is making candied apples and having a *talacho* sell them for me in the yard. The candy apple recipe is pretty simple because it's a box mix from Walmart. Not as easy as you think though, because the instructions are in Spanish. The first batch I ever made was beginners luck because they came out perfect. It was down hill after that. Finally, I got a pastry chef whose in jail with me to help out. Now, as Gwyneth Paltrow would say, "It's all good!"

Artisanal SpongeBob
trash handbag

On sustainability in Mexican Jail

So one day I'm waiting and waiting for the shower. What the fuck is the guy washing in there, a battleship? I have to sneak a peek. He is washing trash. That's right, trash. The wrappers from potato chips and chocolate biscuits and cakes. I found out he makes pocket books and money bags out of them. But goddamn does it take him forever to shower and wash all that trash! I have a guy in my cell that is collecting my empty containers. Every time I finish a bottle of honey, spice, peanut butter, or jelly he is there to get the bottle. Don't know what he does with them all, maybe he uses them in the carpentry shop, but now he is asking me for bottles that aren't even empty! Sheesh! Yes you can have my trash, just let me finish please!

There's this place, called Walmart...

1. They will let you send me money.

2. Ask for a MoneyGram to Cancún.

3. Send the money to Juan.

Look, an asshole!

This Asshole is called Pecho, he's the cell boss. This guy has a nightclub speaker for some reason. This guy hooks it up to the DVD player every day and plays horrible music at an ear-shattering level. Lucky for you, you have earplugs. But then he puts a CD player in the shower on a shelf and turns it all the way up and leaves. Which is why you should always take your earplugs to the shower.

Look, another asshole!

Asshole #2 is the *talacho* called Splinter who is missing part of an ear. Splinter is named after a rat character in a popular kids show about turtles that become ninjas with the help of a rat. This Splinter isn't so cool. When Splinter gets a cold he starts spitting all over the place, including hawking big loogies on the floor while sitting on the toilet. Then he starts spitting in the shower, which would be OK, except he doesn't spit down the drain, so the loogies just stick to the tile. When you complain to the cell boss Splinter's reply is "Well, I put my trash in the sink." What does that have to do with him spitting willy-nilly on the floor? The cell boss, trust me, won't have an answer either.

Whoever considers
the bad luck of the early worm?

I think Franklin Roosevelt said something about that. Even so, make sure to be the early (jail) bird, and try not to think about worms. Wake up daily at around 5:30 AM. It is the best time in Mexican Jail—so very quiet and peaceful that you can hear birds a chirpin', tweetin', and screechin'. It is also good because the other assholes in your cell will still be asleep, except for the *talacho* assigned to cleaning the bathroom. The benefits of waking up early are greater than just the quiet. You can exercise, use the toilet, even cook breakfast, without any people to get in your way. Then you can brush your teeth and you are all set for day. Soon after, you will be welcomed by a cacophony of sounds and smells. Some are seasonal, some are perennial. You can't miss any of these—because you don't have a choice!

Sunrise over Mexican Jail.
Or maybe Sunset.
Does it really matter?

Can't Miss Attractions

Can't Miss	Best Place to Catch it	Peak Season And Time of Day
Bad Breath	Bathroom	Perennial / Morning
Belching	Dinner	Perennial / All day
Chirping bird	Your plancha	Spring / Morning
Cough	Bathroom	Winter / Morning
Fart	Your plancha	Perennial / Morning
Sewer	Bathroom	Summer / All day
Sneeze	Your plancha	Winter / Morning
Snore	Your plancha	Winter / Morning
Spitting	Shower	Winter / Morning
Toilet	Bathroom	Summer / All day
Whacking Off	Your plancha	Perennial / Morning

My cell phone
again!

Ed's crack

Your cell phone can (and will) buy someone else crack.

So Edward knows I have some money and asks to borrow 50 pesos. I know he is going to use the money to buy some crack, so I say no. He begs me and I say no again. He asks to use my phone so he can make some calls and get some phone credits to sell. Edward has done a lot for me so I give him the phone. He leaves, telling me he will be right back. All day long, Edward gives me some bullshit excuse about my phone. Finally, at the end of the day I find out he went straight to the pawn shop and pawned my phone. Fucking motherfucker!! I have to pay $140 pesos the next day to get it back. Of course, the fucking pawn shop guy uses $600 of my credit!! Fucking bastard. Edward and I haven't spoken since.

Rainy days are for laundry (and electrocution)

Rainy days are a great opportunity to catch up on that laundry pile accumulating on your *plancha*. Once I took my wash to the laundry only to find it was closed due to the rain. WTF? Must be nice huh? As I left, I discovered a guy having a seizure, foaming at the mouth, grunting and moaning and rolling all jerky on the ground till they got the gate open to the clinic and four guys carried him away. Now it could have been an act. I'm not a doc and I have never seen a seizure so I don't know for sure. But when I go back to the laundry later it's open again, and I notice a bucket of water with two cables in it plugged into the wall. I ask what's up and the guy says that's how he makes his hot water. Either that, or maybe the laundry room is also where they do their electrocution torture.

Half the fun is getting dolled up!

Did I mention?
Mexican Jail loves to party.

Why? Who knows! But they are always the same: some drag queens oil wrestling, a few drinking contests, followed by the drag queens' dance show, (mainly lap dancing on stage) more drinking contests, then the stripper's raffle. At one party, to make things a little more interesting, they raffled off the drag queens themselves, for an hour in the conjugal, plus some free booze and free drugs. Not too shabby.

We have a woman jail director and she is very supportive of parties. The contests include: who can roll the fastest joint and smoke it while walking in a circle, and who can drink the most *tepache*. Fun stuff like that.

Donald Trump
is a popular choice

Good luck with the Drug Piñata.

Because Mexican Jail has so many good parties, you'll learn about something fun soon enough: the drug piñata. First, everyone stands around the basketball court waiting for the piñata to be raised. They have a little trouble so they bring it down, fix it, then raise it again. The first guy hits it so many times it just breaks before anyone else can have a swing at it. Next thing that happens is that all of the prisoners (say about 1,000 of the 1,500 in the jail) surge forward to get the drugs, candy and fruit. People walk on top of the heads and backs of others to maybe get free drugs. Elbows, fists, and feet go flying. So while it's tough to get a turn swinging at the drug piñata, it's even harder to get the drugs.

wrong kind of pan

⌁ Savvy Prisoner Tip Numero 4: ⌁
Make sure your pan has a handle

A lot of pans in Mexican Jail don't have handles. Someone once told me that was to keep people from using them as weapons. If at all possible, have friends bring you a pan with a handle from the outside. What a difference that makes when cooking breakfast! But even with a handle, the electric stove shoots sparks, so make sure it's a pan with a plastic handle. My cell boss went to make himself a *torta* one morning and when he plugged in the stove to heat it up, the pan, as usual, shot sparks. He got shocked a few more times and more sparks flew but he kept at it until finally it was hot. (He's persistent, which is a good trait in a cell boss.) Then he sat down to eat and dropped the fucking thing on the floor. (He's also kind of clumsy.) Bummer. You can't eat off that floor even using the five second rule. It just isn't safe.

Stuff to do with your crackhead friends

• Hide in the bathroom toilet & peek out when you hear a noise.

• Cuddle yourself.

• Collect pipes – usually just cut from old-fashioned TV rabbit ears.

• Hoard lighters.

Any tool is better
than your fingernails.

I have a friend making me shelves for my *plancha*. I could never cut a straight line and fuck knows how anything in the shop gets cut straight because the table saws are made of wood and the blades are only sort of straight. But as they say in Colombia: any tool is better than your finger nails. The saws have no blade guards either. I'm really surprised that everyone in the shop still has all their fingers, given that there are always lots of people working and bumping into each other. And most everyone has on flip flops, too! My friend has been working on these shelves for four weeks but they are going to turn out great!

TV in Mexican Jail,
with Dials!

Entertainment: Watching commercials

There is a yogurt commercial here that is very funny. It has a group of guys staring at a sexy girl dancer. But the boys' girlfriends don't care because they are staring at a yogurt bottle and the boys can't figure out why. Then the camera shows the bottle, which has a very large strawberry shaped as a tongue. The message is very clear: Strawberry is the best flavor.

FOOD & CULTURE

Inspiration for
the cronut?

Is this a haiku?

A donut and bread
is breakfast three times a week
and dinner on Wednesday.

A chance to
get creative!

∼ Savvy Prisoner Tip ∼
Numero 5:
Visit some shrines
(then maybe make one?)

In Japan they have Shinto shrines. In Thailand (where jail is lots harder) their shrines are called Wats. But it turns out there are also shrines here in Mexican Jail—so cool! And if you want to be like the "hard" guys, you can even make one yourself. Always dedicate your shrine to the grim reaper, otherwise known as "Santa Muerta" or "Saint Death." Be advised the crackheads will all come and smoke crack in front of your shrine. You can decorate it with candles, pictures, statues, bread, candy, and coins. Anytime you go by it, be sure to cross yourself.

Yep.

What's your favorite food? Best not to think about that in Mexican Jail.

The most served food here is hot dogs. They like to call them sausages but they are just fucking hot dogs. Just because you cut a hot-dog up into small pieces doesn't magically turn it into a sausage. They serve hotdogs in pasta as well and I will tell you it sucks as much as you can imagine.

Iranian flag

Mexican Jail will teach you about other cultures (like Iran).

I don't know if this is true because I don't live in, or have ever been to, Iran. But I was looking up sex changes on the internet. (Look, I got nothing else to do and it's not like I'm going to write Beethoven's 9th in here.) So yeah, I wanted to know the process and how all the bits worked. I couldn't find out. But what I did find out was this: Iran has the most sex changes, then it's Thailand. But WTF! Why Iran? Aren't they Muslim? It turns out that's what the closeted gay people do. Change genders! So I guess they don't really have to worry about same sex marriages there because the gay people just change genders. Interesting. I think I would like to go to Iran just to find out if this is true. You can look this up yourself on Wikipedia.

A safe space,
sort of.

If you are a drag queen, you might want to bunk up with the other drag queens.

You'll have more fun that way! You'll know their cell by the pink curtains over the bars. You will have your own boyfriend or you can share one.

Where does the expression "beat the shit out of" come from?

Mexican Jail, probably. Richard is from Canada and is here for 20kgs of marijuana and a few ounces of hash. Richard is such a stoner he has been a drug dealer for 35 years. When he first got here, they wanted him to pay $20,000 USD. He didn't have any money because it was all invested in land or drugs. So they beat him every day, all day, until he actually shat himself. (I checked and the sweet spot to make someone shit is the right side of the gut close to the ribs.)

The Shoe Painter
of Mexican Jail

Guys really obsess about having tidy shoes in Mexican Jail. There is a guy here that paints shoes. Sort of like a shoe shiner but he does touch ups and detailing of the trim of shoes and boots. Makes them look new. The guy is fat and round. Real fat and round. So fat and round that one day I walked by and he wasn't moving. He wasn't dead because he was making a strange noise. It was snoring, which sounded like an asthmatic that just ran a marathon. He is so fat and round that it prevented him from falling forward on to his face even when he was fast asleep!

If you meet a guy
called Sapo…

Sapo means toad. It also means they talk too much, spy, or are tattle tails. It's a bad thing. Anyway this guy must be the ugliest bastard on the planet. He is so ugly I have a hard time comprehending his ugliness. When I am forced to look at him I sometimes think that someone has slipped me some acid as a gag and the acid is really starting to kick in. It also doesn't help that he has a tattoo on his forehead. First, I thought it was a fancy bull's eye but upon further inspection I think it is more a compass rose. Whatever.

Beto's AK?

~ Savvy Prisoner Tip ~
Numero 6:
Be up on the popular music

You'll win friends right away if you rock anything by Norberto "Beto" Quintanilla Iracheta, also known as "El Mero León Del Corrido", which Wikipedia says can be translated as "The Boss Lion Of The Corrido." Guys like Beto write songs called narcocorridos, which are drug ballads. They also pose for pics holding AK-47s in front of their Cadillac Escalades. The narcocorrido is popular in Mexican Jail because they sing about being a Zeta, selling drugs to gringos, having nice cars, big houses, and shootouts with the cops. Sometimes a famous singer will say bad things about the Zetas, and the Zetas kill him. But I'm ok. I have a mini-refrigerator.

LAST THOUGHTS
(MY THUMBS ARE TIRED)

Maybe call your
girlfriend your wife?

The F is the name for the women's prison, and it's basically just another building in Mexican Jail. Everyone here calls their girlfriends their wives. I think the girlfriends do the same for their boyfriends. I think they do it just so you don't get ideas or maybe so you get less ideas. I'd recommend doing it too if you have a special someone.

Drugs are pretty legal here

My Dutch Friend's Mom

Ok, so everyone knows that everyone in jail is innocent right? That includes my Dutch friend, whose name is Free. He was in a fight with the son of a local politician and got pinned for putting the kid in a coma but Free says that isn't the way it went down. Can you believe a word anyone says in jail? Maybe, just maybe. So his mom comes to Mexico to help him get out of jail and instead a blue Ford Mustang pulls up and some guys jump out, grab her and toss her in the car. She is kicking and screaming and someone calls the police. There is a high speed chase and the car crashes. Guys jump out but not all get away. Free's mom is rescued and is ok after the shock wears off. Then the news comes to interview Free and now his story is huge and getting a lot of media coverage in Cancún, Holland, and other European countries! Now Free has a huge chance at freedom!

Am I still in jail?

Yes.

Any day can be a good day, even when the federal court rejects your papers.

You know, I try to always be positive. It is hard to be positive though when you get notified by your lawyer that the federal court is declining to accept your papers. However, I know it's not the end of the world and the lawyer did say it was to be expected. So it's really only mildly depressing. When this happens, it's more important than ever to stick to your daily routines. After two days I was back to my old self! I sort of feel like Jerry Seinfeld sometimes. Kramer said once he was "Even Steven." Every time something bad happens, something good happens too. The longer I stay, the more I learn. Even Steven.

To Recap...

1. Go to Walmart.

2. Ask for a MoneyGram to Cancún.

3. Send the money to Juan and tell him it's for me. You'll be glad you did. Because someone's counting good deeds somewhere. Mother Theresa said something like that...I think.

@unnamedpress

facebook.com/theunnamedpress

unnamedpress.tumblr.com

www.unnamedpress.com

@unnamedpress